THE WEEKEND

A PLAY IN ONE ACT

Melville Lovatt

TSL Drama

First published in Great Britain in 2018
By TSL Publications, Rickmansworth

Copyright © 2018 Melville Lovatt

ISBN / 978-1-912416-24-0

Image courtesy of t0zz at FreeDigitalPhotos.net

The right of Melville Lovatt to be identified as the playwright/author of this work has been asserted by the author in accordance with the UK Copyright, Designs and Patents Act 1988.

All characters and events in this publication, other than those clearly in the public domain, are fictitious and any resemblance to actual persons, living or dead, is purely coincidental.

All rights reserved. No part of this publication may be reproduced, stored in a retrieval system or transmitted, in any form or by any means without the prior written permission of the publisher, nor be otherwise circulated in any form of binding or cover other than that in which it is published and without a similar condition being imposed on the subsequent buyer.

Rights of performance

Rights of performance for this play is controlled by TSL Publications (tslbooks.uk/Drama) which issues a performing licence on payment of a fee and subject to a number of conditions (specified on tslbooks.uk/Drama). This play is fully protected under the Copyright Laws of the British Commonwealth of Nations, the United States of America and all countries of the Berne and Universal Copyright Conventions. All rights, including stage, Motion Picture, Radio, Television, Public Reading and Translation into Foreign Languages are strictly reserved. It is an infringement of the Copyright to give any performance or public reading of this play before the fee has been paid and the licence issued. The Royalty Fee is subject to contract and subject to variation at the sole discretion of TSL Publications. In Territories Overseas the fees quoted may not apply. A fee will be quoted on application to TSL Publications.

THE WEEKEND

A Play In One Act

was first presented as part of
the Harrow Drama Festival
by
Belmont Theatre Company
on
20 July 1998
at
The Travellers Studio Theatre, Harrow Arts Centre

with the following cast:

Clair	Julia Blake
Henry	Adrian Wells
Colin	Michael Collins
Directed by	Melville Lovatt

Running Time

30 minutes

Characters

Clair	*a woman in her early forties*
Henry	*a man in his early forties*
Colin	*a man in his early forties*

Scenes

Scene 1	*The living room. Evening.*
Scene 2	*The living room. Night.*
Scene 3	*The Patio. Next Day. Morning.*
Scene 4	*The beach. Next Day. Afternoon.*

Setting

The stage is divided into three areas.

***DL**, suggested, a small beach. A single sun lounger and one deckchair.*

A blanket spread out on the ground.

***DR**, a living room. A leather swivel chair, UC.*

Two more chairs, DL and DR.

All three chairs should be different in style and design, spare and modern, suggesting affluence.

***Central area**, a patio. Small white table, three chairs.*

An easel and unfinished painting DL.

The patio and beach are in darkness.

Scene 1

Evening. Living room, dimly lit.

COLIN sitting in swivel chair, UC. He is in shadow, his back to audience.

HENRY, standing, stares ahead, DL.

CLAIR sitting, relaxed, DR.

Silence.

HENRY: (*Reflectively.*) Strange.

    Pause.

CLAIR: (*Stares at ceiling.*) Mmmn?

HENRY: Don't you think?

    Pause.

CLAIR: What?

HENRY: All this time?

    Pause.

    Rather strange.

    Pause.

    (*Looks at CLAIR.*) Did he say anything?

CLAIR: No.

HENRY: No ... indication?

    Pause.

CLAIR: Nothing.

HENRY: How long for?

CLAIR: Just the weekend.

HENRY: Uh.

    Pause.

	What time's he coming?
CLAIR:	Around ten.
HENRY:	Ten.
CLAIR:	His train arrives in nine thirty.
HENRY:	I see.

Pause.

I could have met him.

CLAIR:	Mmmn?
HENRY:	At the station?
CLAIR:	Yes. I suggested it.
HENRY:	Oh?
CLAIR:	Said he'd take a taxi.
HENRY:	Uh.

Pause

HENRY starts to whistle. He moves to the chair, stares at it a moment, sits. The whistling stops.

Silence.

How did he sound?

CLAIR:	Sound?
HENRY:	On the phone? I mean, did he ... (*Breaks off.*)
CLAIR:	What?
HENRY:	How did he sound?
CLAIR:	(*Stares at ceiling.*) Just sounded ... well, he ... the same.
HENRY:	Oh.

Slight Pause.

You seem rather uncertain.

CLAIR:	Uncertain?
HENRY:	Of how he sounded?
CLAIR:	We didn't talk for long.

HENRY:	Oh I see. Mmmn.
	Pause.
CLAIR:	His voice sounded ... *samey*. How's that for a word? Samey? Almost as if ... (*Breaks off.*)
HENRY:	What?
CLAIR:	Well ...
HENRY:	Ummn?
CLAIR:	Nothing.
HENRY:	As if what?
CLAIR:	Nothing.
HENRY:	Nothing?
CLAIR:	It's irrelevant.
HENRY:	Irrelevant, eh?
CLAIR:	Yes.
HENRY:	(*Softly, nods.*) So irrelevant you can't tell me.
CLAIR:	Oh for Godsake.
HENRY:	Marvellous.
CLAIR:	(*Looks at him.*) Don't be childish.
HENRY:	Childish?
CLAIR:	Look it isn't ... (*Breaks off.*)
HENRY:	What?
CLAIR:	Important.
HENRY:	(*Brisk, impatient.*) I see.
CLAIR:	His voice was the same. More precise perhaps. Quiet. His impediment wasn't apparent.
	(*Slow, thoughtful.*) No ... he spoke ... very softly.
	(*Smiles.*) His telephone voice.
	It was almost as if he'd ... (*Looks at HENRY.*) never been away.
	Quick fade.
	Lights up.

Scene 2

Living room. Night.
COLIN spins in swivel chair to face front.
All three, sitting, sipping brandy.

CLAIR: (*To COLIN.*) How is it?
COLIN: What?
CLAIR: The brandy?
COLIN: Fine.
CLAIR: Spanish.
COLIN: Really? Quite nice. (*Drains glass.*) Mmmn.
CLAIR: (*Gets up.*) Another?
COLIN: (*Hands empty glass.*) Please.
CLAIR: (*Pours brandy.*) Thought you'd like it
COLIN: (*Nods.*) Not bad.
CLAIR: (*Hands refilled glass.*) Still drink bourbon?
COLIN: (*Smiles.*) You remembered. Ah. Happy days.
CLAIR: (*Smiles, sits as before.*) Ronnie Scott's.
COLIN: Cindy's
CLAIR: Stripes.
COLIN: Samantha's.
CLAIR: Jack's.
COLIN: Ah yes … Jack's.
CLAIR: And Simon's
COLIN: Happy days. (*To HENRY.*) Been back at all?
HENRY: Sorry?
COLIN: To London?

HENRY: No.
COLIN: Never?
HENRY: No. Surprised?
COLIN: No, not really.
HENRY: I'm too busy these days. Far too busy. Expanding. Improving. Keeping up with the times. Keeping up with the fashions...I've ten shops now. Hard work, but rewarding. *Rewarding. Yes.*

The best thing, I think ... as far as my success goes ... isn't, believe it or not, money. Oh no.

The most *satisfying* thing is being in control.

In control of one's own ... in control of one's own ... in control of one's own ... (*Shrugs, small chuckle.*) In control.

Pause.
COLIN: This room ...
CLAIR: What?
COLIN: It's changed.
CLAIR: How?
COLIN: (*Gets up, slowly.*) Seems smaller.
CLAIR: Really?
COLIN: Much smaller.
CLAIR: Oh.
COLIN: (*Stares at ceiling.*) The ceiling ...
CLAIR: (*Stares at ceiling.*) Mmmn?
COLIN: Seems lower.
CLAIR: No.
COLIN: It's *lighter.*
CLAIR: Yes.
COLIN: Yet, lower.

Pause.

(Briskly, turns to CLAIR.) The town's changed.

CLAIR: *(Regretfully.)* Yes.

COLIN: *(Pacing room, slowly.)* Changed a lot. For the worse. All those flats.

(Grimaces.) Terrible. Grotesque. Obscene.

(Briskly, turns to HENRY.) How's Richard?

CLAIR: Fine.

COLIN: *(Turns to CLAIR.)* How old is he now?

CLAIR: Eleven.

COLIN: Eleven.

CLAIR: Nearly twelve.

COLIN: Time flies. I took a taxi to the precinct. Felt like a stroll.

Hellish on the train. Claustrophobic. No seats. Crammed like sardines. Choco-block. Terrible.

I needed a stroll. Took a wander through the town. Ended up on the beach. By the pier.

CLAIR: *(Mildly surprised.)* Oh.

COLIN: *(Nods, smiles.)* Brought back some memories.

CLAIR: *(Smiles.)* Yes it would.

COLIN: *(Short laugh, shakes head.)* Those parties. Seemed like yesterday.

CLAIR: *(Sighs, wistfully.)* Yes …

COLIN: *(Recalls fondly.)* And the sailing …

CLAIR: *(Smiles.)* Yes.

COLIN: The racing!

CLAIR: Yes. You were good. Quite accomplished.

COLIN: *(Modest.)* Wouldn't say that.

CLAIR: Always won.

COLIN: Henry won several times.

CLAIR: Only twice.
COLIN: (*Jovial.*) Cheating.
HENRY: Cheating?
COLIN: (*Gently scolding, as to a child.*) Taking shortcuts. (*Ruffles HENRY'S hair.*) Oh, come on. I'll forgive you. (*Briskly.*) How's your piles? (*Laughs, slowly.*) Sorry. I mean *tiles?*
Turns to CLAIR.
In the kitchen?
CLAIR: Oh, fine.
COLIN: Still got them?
CLAIR: (*Lightly.*) Finest investment we've made.
COLIN: Good. (*Briskly, to HENRY.*) Oh, incidentally, my luggage should arrive. They're sending it on here tomorrow.
HENRY: Oh?
COLIN: (*Starts to go out.*) If I'm out, just sign. Okay?
HENRY: How much is there?
COLIN: Just three. Three cases.
HENRY: You're just staying the weekend?
COLIN: Oh no. I *did* mention there's a slight change of plan?
CLAIR: Yes, you did.
COLIN: (*Yawns, going off.*) I'll say goodnight.
COLIN goes out.
Silence.
HENRY gets up, stands, deep in thought.
He turns, looks at CLAIR.
CLAIR gets up, slowly.
They look at each other.
Silence.
Blackout.

Scene 3

Lights up. Morning. The Patio. Quite sunny.
Coffee, biscuits, two folded newspapers on table.
CLAIR stands, carefully painting her picture.
HENRY stands behind her, watching.
Silence.

HENRY: How long is he staying?
CLAIR: (*Engrossed in painting.*) No idea.
HENRY: Better ask him.
CLAIR: (*Slowly, engrossed.*) Why don't you ask him?
HENRY: Where is he?
CLAIR: Still in bed.
HENRY: Still in bed.
CLAIR: He was tired.
HENRY: On a morning like this?
(*Looks up.*) Not a cloud in … (*Breaks off.*)
Pause.
CLAIR: (*Still engrossed in painting.*) Mmmn?
HENRY: (*Softly, more to himself.*) The sky.
Pause.
COLIN appears, stands, watching and listening.
They are unaware of his presence.
HENRY: The sky …
CLAIR: What about it?
HENRY: Look at it.
CLAIR: (*Looks up.*) Ummn?

HENRY: (*Nostalgically.*) It was like that, that day in the park...
CLAIR: (*Turns back to painting.*) When?
HENRY: Just before we were married.
CLAIR: I've forgotten.
HENRY: Forgotten?
CLAIR: It's a long time ago. I've forgotten.
Pause.
HENRY: I'll refresh your memory. You *painted* the sky.
You insisted on *painting* the sky.
Pause.
You considered it...rare. Its colours...unusual.
You spent all day *painting* the sky.
Pause.
(*Softer.*) Then it rained. We made a dash for it across the green.
You slipped and fell. Remember?
Pause.
When we got there, saturated, the pavilion was locked.
We climbed in through the window. Stripped off. Lit the fire.
Dried ourselves by the fire. (*Softly.*) Made love.
Pause.
No, no I'm wrong. I'm wrong. We didn't.
We didn't make love until later.
Pause.
On a beach. One weekend. You were wearing ... a bikini.
A sleek black bikini ... and sandals.
Pause.

COLIN: Morning.
CLAIR: (*Turns to COLIN.*) Morning. Sleep well?
COLIN: So. So. Nice breakfast.
CLAIR: Enjoy it?
COLIN: (*Sits, right of table.*) Just the ticket.
CLAIR: Good. Like some coffee?
COLIN: Please.
CLAIR: (*Puts down paintbrush.*) Black or white?
COLIN: White.
CLAIR: One sugar?
COLIN: Fine. That's fine.

CLAIR pours three coffees. HENRY stands, watching.
COLIN, relaxed, starts to whistle.

CLAIR: There we are.
COLIN: Ah.
CLAIR: Nice and hot.
COLIN: Good.
CLAIR: (*Sits, at centre of table.*) Help yourselves to biscuits.
COLIN: (*Takes biscuit.*) Think I will. Mmn.

CLAIR crosses her legs.
She sips her coffee, watching HENRY.
HENRY stands.
Pause.
HENRY moves, slowly, to chair, left.
He stares at it a moment, sits.

COLIN: Nice biscuit.
CLAIR: Like them?
COLIN: Quite nice.
CLAIR: Henry's favourites.

COLIN:	(*To HENRY.*) Really?
HENRY:	Wouldn't say that.
CLAIR:	(*To HENRY.*) No?
COLIN:	(*Savours biscuit.*) *Very* nice.
HENRY:	They're not a bad biscuit ... as far as biscuits go.
	They're not a bad biscuit at all. No. But they're not my favourites.
	Never said they were.
CLAIR:	What *are* your favourites?
HENRY:	Fig.
CLAIR:	(*With disbelief.*) Fig?
HENRY:	Fig. Can't beat a good old fig. (*To COLIN.*) How's your wife?
COLIN:	Fine.
HENRY:	Is she coming?
COLIN:	No ... she's away.
HENRY:	Away?
COLIN:	On holiday. The Bahamas.
HENRY:	Good for her.
COLIN:	Yes.
HENRY:	Quite a while since we've seen her. *Love* to see her again.
	Bring her round. A foursome! We'll go out on the town.
	Paint the town. Why not? Have a ball? Rave it up?
	Freak out in The Pig and Whistle. Bring her round.
	Pause.
CLAIR:	(*To COLIN.*) So you slept quite well in our new bed?
COLIN:	Yes, had a strange dream, though.
CLAIR:	Really? What about?

COLIN: Quite strange. (*Relates dream, slowly.*) We were back on the beach.

Walking on the beach. There was no one else around. Not a soul.

No. All was quiet. Almost silent. The sea ... silent ... the sky ... colourless ... silent.

Pause.

We walked, very slowly, through the sand, past the pier, past the first lot of steps ... to the cove.

Pause.

You were wearing ... I think ... yes, I'm sure ... a bikini. A black ... black bikini ... and sandals.

Pause.

(*To HENRY.*) Still play golf?

HENRY: Rarely.

COLIN: Fancy a game?

HENRY: How long are you staying?

COLIN: (*Shrugs.*) Just depends...

CLAIR: Strange ... I was dreaming as well.

COLIN: Last night?

CLAIR: Yes. Something moving around in my eye.

Pause.

HENRY: (*Softly, impatient, rising to his feet.*) What was it, for Godsake?

CLAIR: I lay quite still. Lay waiting until it went to sleep.

Pause.

Then I took it out, slowly. Held it in my hand.

Pause.

HENRY: (*Brisk, impatient.*) And?

CLAIR: (*Smiles, to HENRY.*) Three guesses.

HENRY:	No idea.
CLAIR:	Guess.
HENRY:	Haven't a clue.
CLAIR:	Three guesses.
HENRY:	No idea.
CLAIR:	(*Smiles.*) Just *guess*.
HENRY:	(*Bending over CLAIR, close to her.*) A rabbit? A snake? A tortoise? A tiger? A kangaroo? A chimpanzee? A stoat? A rat?
CLAIR:	(*Smiles.*) No.
HENRY:	(*Faster.*) A squirrel? A fox? A ferret? A parrot? A falcon? Hedgehog? Camel? Giraffe?
CLAIR:	No.
HENRY:	(*Faster still, face savage.*) A moth? Beetle? Cockroach? Spider? Earwig? Elephant? Crocodile? Crab?
CLAIR:	No.
COLIN:	A snail?
CLAIR:	(*Smiles, surprised.*) Correct.
HENRY:	(*Brisk, turns to COLIN.*) I was dreaming as well.
COLIN:	Oh really? What a coincidence.
HENRY:	Yes. I dreamt of *your* wife. Alone. Bored. Bored out of her mind with palm trees, sand, sea, rocks, beautiful people. Let's put it on the table. I mean, *won't* she be lonely? Won't she be missing you? Out there on her own?
COLIN:	She's very independent.
HENRY:	Of course she's independent...
COLIN:	She has *other* interests.
HENRY:	(*Sharp.*) That's not the point.

COLIN: You seem to be getting your knickers in a twist.
CLAIR: Sit down Henry.
COLIN: Yes, why not sit down?
HENRY: (*Patiently, to CLAIR.*) I don't want to sit down.
COLIN: Then by all means, stand.
HENRY: (*Softly, to COLIN.*) Well, thanks.
COLIN: Not at all.
CLAIR: (*To HENRY.*) Why not go for a walk?
HENRY: A walk?
CLAIR: You seem restless.
HENRY: I'm not at all restless.
CLAIR: You seem rather tense.
HENRY: (*Sharp.*) I'm not at all tense.
COLIN: (*Suddenly alarmed, gets up.*) Oh no!
CLAIR: What's the matter?
COLIN: (*Desperately dodging a bee.*) A bee. A bee. I can't stand them. I was badly stung as a kid. Look, where is it, now?
CLAIR: (*Getting up.*) Careful.
COLIN: W-Where is it?
CLAIR: On your shoulder. Stand still.

Pause.

COLIN: Has it gone?
HENRY: There's another.
COLIN: Another?
CLAIR: On your head.
COLIN: (*Trembling.*) C-Can't stand them.
HENRY: (*Cheerfully.*) They seem to *like* you.

(*Softly, grabs a newspaper.*) Stand still.

CLAIR: Henry, *don't*.

HENRY:	(*Softly, to COLIN, raises newspaper to strike.*) Stand still.
CLAIR:	Henry, look … just leave them.
COLIN:	(*Trembling violently.*) J-Just leave them.
HENRY:	(*With relish, about to strike.*) I'll soon have them off.
CLAIR:	(*Relieved.*) They've gone.
	Pause.
COLIN:	(*Great sigh of relief.*) Phew!
HENRY:	(*Chuckles.*) They're back!
CLAIR:	(*Irritably, dodging bees.*) Oh no.
COLIN:	(*To CLAIR, grabs newspaper.*) C-Careful …
HENRY:	(*Confidently, to CLAIR.*) They'll go.
CLAIR:	In my hair…
HENRY:	(*Chuckles.*) Look, don't panic.
COLIN:	(*Points.*) There it is.
HENRY:	(*Turns to look.*) Where?
COLIN:	(*Strikes with newspaper on HENRY'S neck.*) Got it!
HENRY:	(*Clutches neck.*) Aaaaaahh!
	HENRY stands, moaning, clutching his neck.
	COLIN sinks into chair, wiping brow with handkerchief.
COLIN:	(*Unwell, unfastening shirt collar.*) Oh Lord.
CLAIR:	(*Curious, rather than concerned, to COLIN.*) You alright?
COLIN:	(*Wiping brow.*) I feel sick. Feel sick. Feel ghastly.
CLAIR:	(*Hands coffee to COLIN.*) Drink your coffee.
HENRY:	(*Moans, clutching his neck.*) Oh God.
COLIN:	(*Gulps coffee.*) That's better.
	HENRY groans.
COLIN:	(*'Sick' again, wipes brow.*) So hot…

CLAIR: You've gone white.
COLIN: Feel sick ...
CLAIR: Just relax.
COLIN: (*Fans himself with newspaper.*) That's better.
CLAIR: Feel better now?
COLIN: (*Nods, recovered.*) Yes.
HENRY: (*Sharply, to CLAIR.*) Look, what about me? I'm the one who's been stung.
CLAIR: (*Impatiently, moves to HENRY.*) Stand still.
HENRY: (*Anxiously, as CLAIR touches, examines his neck, closely.*) What you doing?
CLAIR: Removing the sting.
HENRY: (*Almost shrill.*) Look be careful, for Godsake ...
CLAIR: (*Very firmly.*) Still.

Pause.

(*Removes bee sting.*) There, it's out.
COLIN: So sorry old chap.
HENRY: Sorry?
CLAIR: (*To both men.*) More coffee?
COLIN: (*Hands cup to CLAIR.*) Please.

Pause.

CLAIR pours COLIN coffee.

HENRY stands, watching.

COLIN sips coffee.

HENRY rubs sore neck.

CLAIR sits as before, crossing her legs.

COLIN stares at the sky.

HENRY watches them.
CLAIR: I read somewhere that when a bee stings, it dies.

COLIN: Is that so?

CLAIR: It actually dies.

COLIN: There you are then, Henry, in a manner of speaking, that bee died for *you*.

HENRY: It didn't die for *me*. It *didn't* die for me, did it?

It made no decision. It made no decision to sting me and die.

You killed it. You swotted it. Snuffed out it's life.

COLIN: Would have stung you anyway.

HENRY: How do we know?

COLIN: It was hovering over you.

HENRY: Bees *always* hover.

COLIN: Close. Very close to you.

HENRY: Bees *hover* close! Mean, they're *famous* for hovering bloody close!

COLIN: Well, I'm sorry. I'm sorry. What more can I say?

CLAIR: (*To HENRY.*) He *was* trying to stop it stinging you.

COLIN: Yes ...

CLAIR: His intentions were ...

HENRY: Honourable?

CLAIR: Good. They were good.

HENRY: Well, the road to hell's paved with them.

CLAIR: (*Very firmly, stands, hands him coffee.*) Coffee.

Pause.

HENRY takes coffee from her. He slowly sits.

CLAIR sits again, crossing her legs.

Pause.

COLIN: Gone duller now.

CLAIR: Mmmn.

COLIN: The forecast said rain.

Pause.

Gone distinctly dark.

Pause.

The Met men these days are usually right.

(*To HENRY, with almost cheerful conviction.*) Yes ... rain it will.

Pause.

HENRY: I don't think it will. In fact, it won't. I'm categorically sure it won't.

The Met men are idiots. Bloody clowns. Rain? No way.

CLAIR: (*Softly.*) Might.

Pause.

COLIN: (*Reflectively.*) The sky ...
CLAIR: Sorry?
COLIN: Reminds me of our picnic.
CLAIR: Picnic?
COLIN: Remember?
CLAIR: I'm afraid I don't.
COLIN: Out in Hastings one weekend. You *painted* the sky.
CLAIR: Out in Hastings?
COLIN: Oh surely you remember ...
CLAIR: No.
COLIN: But you painted ...
HENRY: (*Briskly, to COLIN.*) She *doesn't* remember.
COLIN: Amazing.
HENRY: It's pointless discussing it further.
COLIN: Strange ...
HENRY: It's absolutely pointless.
COLIN: (*To CLAIR.*) You honestly don't ...

CLAIR:	(*Stands, slowly.*) I remember something else though …
COLIN:	What?
CLAIR:	I remember childhood. When we were small.
	Hide and seek by the rocks. Our favourite game.
	Once I hid inside the cliff. Remember? The opening inside the cliff?
	A tiny cave. It was warm and dry and safe from the sea.
	Outside you were searching. Calling my name.
	Your voices far away. Distant. Remote.
	Pause.
	Miles away.
	Pause.
	You were nowhere near me. Either of you.
	You were never, at any time, anywhere near.
	You never did find me.
COLIN:	In fact, I did.
CLAIR:	I gave myself up. Grew bored with my cave.
COLIN:	I played the waiting game. *Knew* you'd grow bored.
	Pause.
	Stands, faces CLAIR.
	I knew you'd grow bored.
	Pause.
	Let's face it, you couldn't have stayed in your cave.
CLAIR:	No?
COLIN:	(*Small chuckle.*) You'd have died. You had to come out.
	Just a question of waiting. As simple as that.
	Pause.

	You had to come out.
CLAIR:	Yes. Yes, you're right. I had to…had to come out.

I came out, briefly, into the sun.

(*Looks at HENRY.*) Then followed Henry into a different cave.

Pause.

A much larger cave.

Pause.

Turns away, looks out front.

If it's sunny tomorrow, I'll go to the beach.

So long since I've been there. I'll lie in the cove.

I'll get brown all over. All over … brown. Mmn. Should be nice.

Blackout.

Lights up.

Scene 4

Sunny beach. The next day. Afternoon.
The deckchair is in the shade.
CLAIR, sitting on the sun lounger, applies lotion to her arms.
She wears a black bikini and sandals.
HENRY stands, looking tense, staring out front.
He wears Bermudas and sandals.
Silence.
HENRY turns, looks at CLAIR.
CLAIR lies back, slowly, closing her eyes.
She lies still.
Silence.
HENRY turns, slowly, stares out as before.
He turns, looks at CLAIR who lies still.
Silence.

HENRY: Look, I've been thinking. You're right? Okay? You're right. Spot on. You're perfectly right.
(*Emphatically.*) From now on ... that's *it*. Things will be different.
I promise. I promise you things *will* change.
For a start, no more travelling. I'll cut it all out.
Expansion? Who needs it? I've ten bloody shops.
Who needs more expansion? Ten shops is enough.
Who needs more, for Godsake? No, ten shops is fine.
I mean, the main thing is *remain in control*.
Keep it small. Keep it tight. Keep it small, keep it tight,

I can oversee, monitor ... monitor, mould. Get too big ... I've lost it.

Anyway, well ... that's it. I mean, things ... things *will* ... *will* change.

No more running around like a blue arsed fly.

There'll be more time together. More time to ourselves.

Pause.

More *time* to ourselves.

Pause.

Look, how about ... having a night out tonight?

A meal, then on to the cinema?

Pause.

Or a meal, then on to the theatre, if you like. A meal, then on to the theatre?

Pause.

Pygmalion's on at the moment, I think. Your favourite.

Old George Bernard Shaw.

Pause.

Well, you're always complaining we never go out. How about going out?

Pause.

Going out tonight?

Pause.

How about going out tonight?

Silence.

CLAIR lies very still.

HENRY turns, slowly, stares out as before.

Silence.

HENRY turns, looks back at CLAIR.

She lies still.

HENRY moves nearer to her.

HENRY: Look, why don't …?
Pause.
I mean, *why* don't …?
Pause.
Why don't we take a holiday or something?
Pause.
Get away from it all? A month in Athens?
What would you say to that?
Pause.
Two months away. We could make it two.
Two months or … even three.
Pause.
A three month *cruise*! That's just the ticket!
A three month luxury cruise.
Pause.
Of course, it doesn't … doesn't *have* to be a cruise.
Look, the choice is yours. I'll go anywhere you like.
I mean, just name a place. Say the word and we'll go.
Pause.
Just name a place and we'll go.
Pause.
Listen, I've been thinking, about this …
Pause.
Just say the word and we'll go!
Pause.
I mean, which … which would …

(*Half sobs, sinks to his knees, next to CLAIR.*) which would you prefer?

Pause.

Softly, closes eyes, clutches side of sun lounger.

 Which ... which *would* you ...?

CLAIR lies, back to HENRY.

HENRY kneels.

Silence.

COLIN appears, wears Bermudas.

CLAIR sits up.

CLAIR: (*To COLIN.*) How's the sea ?
COLIN: Quite warm.
CLAIR: Only quite warm?
COLIN: Warm. Aren't you coming in?

Pause.

You said you'd come in. Said you'd follow me in.

CLAIR: (*Lies as before, her back to both men.*) Maybe later.

CLAIR stretches her legs, lies still.

HENRY kneels.

COLIN stands.

Silence.

Fade.

By Melville Lovatt

Full Length Plays

Small Mercies	Comedy-Drama	4M	2F
The Powers That Be	Thriller	3M	3F + 1 boy
Visiting Time	Family Drama	3M	2F
Desperate Measures	Dark Comedy	3M	1F

One Act Plays

Accommodation	Tragicomedy	4M	1F
The Lamp	Comedy-Drama	1M	1F
The Distressed Table	Comedy-Drama	1M	1F + Voiceover (F)
The Boomerang	Comedy-Drama	3M	1Boy + Voiceover (F)
Making Adjustments	Comedy-Drama	1M	2F
The Kiss	Thriller	2M	1F
The Weekend	Drama	2M	1F
The Grave	Drama	2M	

Monologue Collections

Standing Alone (16 monologues)	Comedy-Drama	8M	8F

All enquiries to TSL Publications: www.tslbooks.uk

www.ingramcontent.com/pod-product-compliance
Lightning Source LLC
Chambersburg PA
CBHW071804040426
42446CB00012B/2712